TWO FOLK SONGS

To the city

When you're all alone,
and life is making you lonely,
you can always go — DOWNTOWN.

When you've got worries,
all the noise and the hurries
seem to help, I know — DOWNTOWN.

Just listen to the music of the
traffic in the city,
linger on the sidewalk,
the neon lights are pretty.
How can you lose?

The lights are much brighter there,
you can forget all your troubles,
forget all your care,
so go — DOWNTOWN.

It will be great when you're
DOWNTOWN,
No finer place for sure
DOWNTOWN,
Everything's waiting for you.

Tony Hatch

Cover

The new city must arise out of the old, as an extension of its spirit, or as a replacement of a worn-out
part. Here the image is made up of fragments of
designs used in the Fulham Study, with which the
author was associated, superimposed on an air photo
of Fulham.
Aerofilms Ltd

Frontispiece

Bryant Park and Public Library, New York

To the suburb

Little boxes on the hillside,
Little boxes made of ticky-tacky,
Little boxes, little boxes, little boxes
All the same.

There's a green one, and a pink one,
And a blue one and a yellow one,
And they're all made out of ticky-tacky,
And they all look just the same.

And the people in the houses
All go to the university,
And they all get put in boxes, little boxes,
All the same.

And there's doctors and there's lawyers,
And there's business executives,
And they're all made out of ticky-tacky,
And they're all just the same.

And they all play on the golf course
And drink their Martini dry,
And they all have pretty children
And the children go to school.

And the children go to summer camp
And then to the university,
And they all get put in boxes
And they come out the same.

And the boys go into business
And marry and raise a family,
And they all get put in boxes, little boxes,
All the same.

There's a green one, and a pink one,
And a blue one and a yellow one,
And they're all made out of ticky-tacky,
And they all look just the same.

Malvina Reynolds

Architecture: city sense

Theo Crosby

Studio Vista London
Reinhold Publishing Corporation
New York

Architecture : City Sense

A Studio Vista/Reinhold Art Paperback
Edited by John Lewis
© Theo Crosby 1965
Reprinted 1967
Published in London by Studio Vista Limited
Blue Star House, Highgate Hill, London N19
and in New York by Reinhold Publishing Corporation
430 Park Avenue, New York
Library of Congress Catalog Card Number 65-14036
Set in 9/11 Univers Medium 689
Printed in the Netherlands
by N.V. Drukkerij Koch & Knuttel, Gouda
SBN : 289.27989.5

Contents

Preface The number of people concerned with our environment is dishearteningly small, and they are divided by many parochial quarrels. In the face of the great, essentially new, environmental problems of the next fifty years, these conflicts have now little relevance. Our civilisation, poised uneasily between affluence and oblivion, now demands a great and positive gesture, a great leap forward, to provide a new way of life for all the world's citizens. This new concept must utilise our fantastic technological potential, welcome and provide for the vast numbers of new citizens who will soon be with us, creatively enjoy the coming opportunities for leisure and for individual self realisation.

This way of life will largely depend on planning and architectural inventions, which must be formulated **now.** This book makes no claim to originality; it attempts to synthesise ideas from many sources into a coherent approach to city planning, with the basic assumption that city life is desirable and exciting. It is an assumption, long unfashionable in planning circles, shared by most of the human race.

Empire State Building, New York.

'Adoration of the Magi', whalebone 1120. *Victoria and Albert Museum, London. Crown copyright*

Visual order and disorder

The only thing that distinguishes man from other animals is his capacity to create order. From the ability to identify and name things, he has been able to sort them into controllable categories. Once a thing, a bird or flower, has been named it is in our power: we can open a file on it, note its habits and weaknesses, publish a monograph, thus explaining to others of our kind how to perpetuate our control over it.

Primitive cultures knew the power of a name. Those things most sacred were not named, or were given secret or gulling names, which were passed on only to initiates. There are thus two kinds of knowledge: a general and accepted public knowledge which reflects the state of popular education, and specialised knowledge which is particular to a certain priesthood, art or craft.

Renaissance stage setting.

Peruvian textile

This situation exists in the case of visual or plastic* knowledge. There is a popular knowledge, based on things *seen*, and an esoteric knowledge based on things *known*. Esoteric knowledge is gradually diffused into the general culture. For example the public knows about perspective in a general way, because its effects can be perceived once the eye has been prepared for it by an elaborate education. It is now part of our culture to know about perspective. We therefore *see* things in perspective.

But the understanding of the visual system, and the method of drawing a perspective view of a building or a landscape, is even today a specialised knowledge, based on an esoteric geometric and mathematical discipline. That is something *known*.

There are many other examples that might be quoted of visual knowledge, though perspective is particularly interesting in being such a late discovery, and one confined to western civilisation. It was invented in the thirteenth century, and there exist many paintings of earlier periods, or other cultures, which use other systems. (A field, for example, on which objects of greater or lesser importance are placed, according to a two dimensional geometry, and shown enlarged or reduced according to their social, political or religious status).

---

* Dealing with the three dimensional arts of architecture and sculpture.

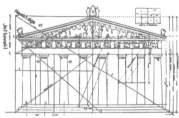

The Parthenon, Athens, with proportional analyses according to Hambidge, Moessel, Joltowski and Ghyka

There has always been a corpus of esoteric visual knowledge, or at the very least a series of recipes for particular effects. Based on elementary geometry and the relationship of simple numbers, this has always been intricately linked with religious and philosophical theory.* On this base was erected the greatest monuments of the civilisations of the Egyptians, Greeks and Romans: an architecture of often incredible invention, subtlety and refinement. Our knowledge of the details of the system used by the Greeks and Romans is limited: some of it is based on archaeological research, and what little can be found in surviving classical or mediaeval documents. In fact Vitruvius's treatise is the only surviving classical architectural document; and, full of good sense though it is on more mundane matters, there is practically nothing about proportion or theory.

---

* For a detailed exposition of this theme, see Scholfield's *The Theory of Proportion in Architecture;* Scully's *The Earth, the Temple and the Gods;* Rykwert's *The Idea of a Town.*

'Deposition' by Raphael. *Borghese Gallery, Rome*. Analysis by the author

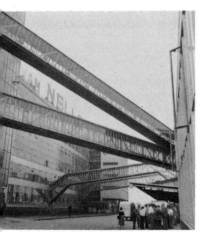

Van Nelle factory, Rotterdam 1927. An example of the new mode of architectural composition developed in the twenties

This was deduced, mainly from measuring classic remains, by a series of architects of the Renaissance, from Alberti and Palladio to Serlio. Under the influence of the current philosophy of Neo-Platonism, they constructed from the measured data proportional systems that reflected the musical, mathematical and religious aspirations of the time. By the eighteenth century, though, proportional theory had become exceedingly complex, and somewhat unreal, and was swept away by the general revolt against classic discipline, the romantic movement.

The artists and architects of the nineteenth and twentieth century were not ignorant of these theories, but as they could not share their sixteenth-century religious and philosophic basis, the theories seemed to them irrelevant. However they continued to use the systems while looking about for a new theoretical basis*. The discoveries of the Impressionists and Cubists, and the manifestoes of the Futurists produced a new and entirely fluid conception of visual reality. The Impressionists were concerned with effects of light, with informal composition; the Cubists with transparency, simultaneity, the construction of images from disparate elements; the Futurists with technology, speed and social change.

Architecture followed, as always, some little way behind the painters, but here these various preoccupations joined with a new technology of steel, concrete and glass to produce an entirely new mode of building.

A new theory of architectural composition was also produced. Classic systems are, like classic structures, closed systems, symmetrical and finite. The new architecture was asymmetrical, open ended, not precisely calculable. The conflict between the two systems has still to be resolved, but the key buildings, which stated and in part resolved the problems, were built in the twenties.

The new architecture of the twenties was an architecture of symbol (for the designers asked too much of contemporary technology, so that few buildings survive unscathed) and of didactic experiment. Yet even these buildings owe a great deal

---

* This search is described in Peter Collins's *Changing Ideals in Modern Architecture*.

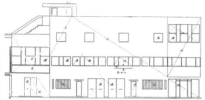

Left: analysis of Maison La Roche, Paris 1923 by Le Corbusier.
Above: office building, London 1920.
Below left: Heathcote, Ilkley, Yorkshire 1906, both by Sir E. Lutyens.
Below: midtown New York, a heritage of splendid, intelligent buildings carelessly eroded

to classical proportional systems. Their determined asymmetry is governed by 'regulating lines'. These buildings are 'literate' in the same sense, at the same time, and in almost exactly the same way as those of Sir Edwin Lutyens, a most esoteric proportioneer.

We have tended to lose this literacy in the great expansion of architectural production since the war: with so many thousands of young architects and vast numbers of new buildings, it has become somewhat diluted.

Literacy is what makes the difference between a good and a bad building, as it does between literature and journalism. The standard of most bad building is even lower than the poorest journalism, for the journalist, or his proof reader, at least knows elementary grammar and spelling.

The great, and increasing, areas of speculative housing, of poor and unimaginative local authority building are the greatest threat to our environment. Cities spread, in spite of planners, into the countryside, and they do so in a haphazard and disorderly way. Most of this building is organised and built by the visually illiterate: the speculative builder and developer, the city valuer or the borough engineer.

The first step to any resolution of the problem is the removal of the amateur from the control of building or planning. Buildings must all be designed by qualified architects, and these must raise their standards to a decent literacy. On this basis the larger problems of environment can be tackled; without it very little will be accomplished.

Office building in New York, an effective adaptation of Gothic systems to a tall building.
Below: 'City of Cathedrals' after Paul Klee

Cities

The city is man's greatest invention : an intellectual powerhouse, a store of learning and of the most diverse energies. Cities and civilisation are synonymous. Nothing can replace the essential civilising function of the individual and group contacts, the face-to-face meeting, the net of groups, societies and associations that make up the most valued part of each individual's life. Only a city provides a sufficient cross section of society for everyone, however specialised, to find a friend. In short, while in a village or suburb you may know everybody, the people you *want* to know can only be found in the city.

Our society becomes constantly more educated and more specialised; the growth of cities into great conurbations is somehow part of our general intellectual expansion. We need to be near each other. As industries increase in size and complexity they need more skilled, and more specialised labour, and workers must live near their work. A skilled man rightly insists on a possibility of choice of work, and also of recreation. Choice is only available in a city ; the larger the city the wider the choice.

It is argued that improved communications and greater physical mobility will disperse the city, and dissolve the need for its concentration. This never happens, the city's tentacles stretch a little further with each improvement, and the need for contact, in work and play, remains.*

There is, of course, an optimum size for everything, and the great cities of the world are now too big to function efficiently, because their original infrastructure of roads and services is obsolete. For example, London is expected to function with a central area road and services system provided in the eighteenth and nineteenth centuries, though the population has grown from 2,7 million in 1850 to 8,1 million in 1960, and the built area from 100 sq. miles to over 600 sq. miles. New York has grown into an urban region containing 14,5 million people, all focussed on Wall Street, and a small section of midtown. In

* Cars, telephones represent not so much a new and higher standard of life as a means of clinging to something of the old. Where you could walk to your enjoyment you did not need a car ! *Family and Kinship in East London*, Wilmot & Young.

spite of this obvious disadvantage, every year the population of a new town (60,000 people) comes to London, because London (like New York) is a *place*, the place to be, the place where things happen, the place where the money is. A migration like this is not to be easily diverted, particularly since the drift to large cities is a movement of talent. The big city attracts, above all, the talented and ambitious, the adventurous, the most valuable elements of our society. Their presence and their interaction make the city an infinitely varied and exciting place.

The city, too, has the virtue that it provides a proper relationship between private and public life. In a city one is not anonymous for very long. There is a fine network of public involvement with local tradesmen and neighbours, greetings, noddings and occasional exchanges, while the basic privacy of the individual is undisturbed. Public life is further extended in work and recreational association, so that an individual is always within a web of contacts, of infinite variety and degree, each of which produces responses and involvements. These involvements create, ultimately, social responsibility, and are a most valuable social education. Unless each citizen is able to participate fully in this complex world, to feel himself part of it, and responsible to it, his life is lonely and he remains undifferentiated.

For everyone wants to be somebody, needs an identity. Identity is a complex phenomenon, but one acquires it by virtue of action, appearance, and above all, involvement. The city is the great stage, the citizens actors; each one has a role to play in the drama of everyday life.

In architectural terms, it is important that buildings should promote identity: that is, the individuality of each citizen. They should also promote social involvement, the opportunity for contact at every level, and thus help towards the efficient functioning of the city, and the social education of the citizen.

Like individuals, cities should have character and flavour; like individuals, this flavour is made up of numerous characteristics, or identifiable elements. Thus a city made up of regular-width streets with only single storey bungalows as a fabric would tend to lack character, and the inhabitants would suffer from it.

The poetry of cities — left: downtown New York.
Below: an English New Town

The outskirts of Florence: the mode of building allows an infinite variety of form and accommodation.
Below: a Birmingham suburb

Cities with a variety of street scene, of road width, of building height and function, even when they are ugly, are a source of joy and pride to their inhabitants. Because they have *identity*. They contain recognisable elements, towers, squares, domes and spires which are readily apprehended, which serve as landmarks, and which help to differentiate the parts of the city.

Cities which act in this way are almost always old cities, where identifiable buildings have accreted over the years. New towns, because of their newness, and their separation of functions, lack identifiable elements. Old cities are all mixed up; housing, shopping, offices, workshops are all in the same street, often in the same building. This makes for that unity in diversity, the complexity which is the essence of living in cities. Once functions are separated, the city goes to pieces.

One might therefore produce an axiom that a city, or a section of a city, does not depend on its size, but on its arrangement. Given every possible function, the city will create and sustain itself. Given only one function it will inevitably decay, as witness the blight on the inner ring of housing in most cities. Note also how the blight spreads outwards as fast as the new outer suburbs are constructed.

A city must be able to regenerate itself, to heal its own tissue, to retain its values so that it remains economic gradually to rebuild and renew its buildings. This is partly a problem of economics, partly of sociology, partly of politics, partly of architecture. No city can be held together entirely by its architecture, and Venice is the exception which proves the rule.

A city made for walking — Patras. Below: musicians in Archer Street, London, a ritual gathering constantly interrupted by vehicles

The architect is not a prime mover in the city or any other situation. He is a technician who does what is asked of him by his clients. He will try to create something of value within an existing situation, but he is seldom allowed to create the situation. Yet a building, once built, becomes a factor in any environmental equation, and its form and usage has an incalculable effect on its surroundings: promoting or inhibiting renewal, raising or lowering land values, intensifying or decreasing social activity. The end result of the architect's work is often important, though it is seldom to be foreseen in advance.

The vagaries of the user, which bring an architectural pattern to

A city of stubby office blocks — Croydon. *Photo Aerofilms Ltd*

A city of sprawling two storey housing, and its complement (below) of
standard factories — Hemel Hempstead. *Photos Aerofilms Ltd*

life, are seldom predictable, though we are beginning to understand something of the complex working of cities. Our knowledge can only come from observation of existing situations, preferably over a long period of time. Some primarily sociological studies in Britain and the U.S. have gone a long way towards undermining planning preconceptions. From even a cursory examination of existing towns and what has been done to them in recent years, it is obvious that most of our planning theory is wrongly based. Most of this theory was put forward to counter a problem that has now ceased to exist. Up to 1939 the problem was poverty: the eradication of slums and the other social consequences of poverty. The slums were overcrowded, houses very close together, with many activities mixed together in the same area. Therefore, to cure the situation, it was argued that these conditions should be reversed: people decentralised, houses spread apart, functions separated. Then the slums would automatically disappear.

Diagrams from a study by Walter Gropius showing how tall buildings provide equivalent accommodation and more free ground area than low structures. From this diagram to the control of height and form by the light angle mechanism was a short step.
Below: project for Berlin 1930 by L. Hilbersheimer

In the complex equation that equals a city, this elementary reasoning has resulted in a nightmarish sprawl of housing, a concentration of offices in the old centres, endless journeys to work, or for recreation, or for that specialised human contact that is the city's greatest gift.

The simple rules invented by Walter Gropius to guide planners as to the amount of sunlight which should reach each dwelling, have been made into a conscious system for producing certain kinds of desert: the city of stubby commercial office blocks, with prestige entrances islanded from each other by a sea of cars and asphalt; a city of sprawling two-storey housing with no end, no beginning; with standard roads, standard verges, standard gardens. The complement to these two environments is the factory estate, with a maze of standard factories standing amid piles of junk which no-one bothers to tidy away.

No-one can fail to recognise that our environment becomes more and more like this, from one end of Britain to the other, and that the same pattern exists in the U.S. (where the houses have only one storey and stand a little farther apart).

It all looks the same, mainly because of the separation of functions, and the blind adherence to a set of rules made for a problem that has already disappeared.

Affluence, not poverty, is the problem of the sixties. Twenty years of technical and social progress have changed the situation. No longer must cities be rebuilt to alleviate chronic housing conditions; they must be regenerated to provide for the high and growing aspirations of a young, plump and greedy new generation. The city of the newly affluent must be full of old world virtues. That is, it must be visually and socially dynamic, or the citizen uses his new found mobility to move to some place that has these virtues, and by his alien presence destroys them. This is what is happening to the big cities, to the coastal towns of southern Britain and the Mediterranean, as the affluent alien moves, in quantity, to claim his share.

The port of Hydra

Order and responsibility

Perhaps the only way that visually and socially dynamic cities can be brought about is by the correct marshalling of constructive forces. Of these the most potent, and easily achieved, is a hierarchy of planner, architect, artist.

One of the basic tenets of the modern movement has been the interrelation of the arts: the need to bring back painting and sculpture from the museums and galleries into a close and vital relationship with architecture. In many conferences artists and architects have stood up to demand from each other a close collaboration for the creation of great new works, a kind of visual opera which would harmoniously knit the divergent tendencies of our time into a unity. This unity would also be a social force.

This splendid ambition remains unrealised, though of course there is plenty of precedent in history for such a collaboration, where the work of artist and architect merge into a synthesis, and where the total effect transcends the limitations of either art. Late Baroque or Rococo churches are most often quoted, but examples can be found in all periods and cultures: the painted sculptures on Greek temples, Hindu temples covered with carving, Mexican pyramids. In fact, all ancient building incorporated certain elements of sculpture and painting as a norm. Only in the nineteenth century did the artist become completely separated from the architect, and look entirely to the private patron to support him. Patronage became important during the Renaissance, when the idea of survival after death through art became a basic Humanist belief. The artist, after centuries of working as a more or less anonymous craftsman for the glory of God and the Church, found that he could convey immortality. His price was to be valued as an individual, somehow separate from and above society.* By the late nineteenth century no serious artist would concern himself with the vulgar problems of building. By this time the architect too had almost divorced himself from the problem, and was concerned, like most of the painters, with history and style. He was not involved with

---

* 'I feel strongly that the artist has no responsibility to the community'. Mr. Robert Motherwell 1963.

Above left: the Renaissance concept of space as static — fresco by Pin-turriclio *(Cathedral Library, Siena)*; and the twentieth-century mode of spatial organisation, fluid and dynamic — Léger's 'Three Women' 1921 *(Collection, The Museum of Modern Art, New York. Mrs Solomon Guggen-heim Fund)* and (below) the Bauhaus, Dessau by Walter Gropius 1925

Turner's 'Snowstorm' 1842. *Courtesy National Gallery, London*

Paxton's Crystal Palace 1851. *Victoria and Albert Museum, London. Crown copyright.* Below: project for the headquarters of Pravda, Moscow 1920 by the Vesnin brothers

techniques, and was overtaken by the engineers with such buildings as the Crystal Palace, the great railway bridges, the warehouses of London and Liverpool. These buildings were not considered 'architecture' even by their designers. Yet their logic, economy and strength soon transformed architecture, and the modern movement is basically an attempt by architects to understand and control the incredible capacity of new building technology.

During the nineteenth century some painters began to lose their preoccupation with history and began to study nature and science. Problems of light were absorbing scientists like Davy, Faraday and Edison, and also fascinated Turner and the Impressionists. The invention of cheap glass, and improvements in cast iron, made possible the Crystal Palace, a building very close in spirit, and in effect, to Turner's late paintings.

Basic themes often make themselves felt, contemporaneously, across several disciplines. The Cubists were concerned with several interesting visual problems: simultaneity, transparency, the ambivalence of 'reality', of actual and simulated materials, and the construction of images from fractional elements each carrying perhaps an overtone of disparate meaning. Their activity owed a good deal to contemporary poets, philosophers and mathematicians, and deeply affected a generation of architects.

From this intellectual ferment, some basic architectural solutions began to emerge in the twenties. For example, Mies van der Rohe produced the idea of the glass towers that forty years later have transformed cities all over the world. A new method of architectural composition was established, using the integration or juxtaposition of disparate elements, each expressing a different function or message, to build a powerful and complex image. A new way of thinking about structure: skeletal, with 'curtain' walls. A new way of organising space: a continuum modelled and shaped by planes, transparent or opaque.

All these ideas cohere into a mode of perceiving and designing completely opposed to traditional systems. Modern art and architecture are fundamentally related: they have evolved from a common matrix of ideas. Some painters have influenced architects very directly: Léger, for example, contributed vastly to Le Corbusier's buildings without painting a single wall for

him. Mies van der Rohe owes much to Paul Klee. But in general, artists and architects have grown apart in forty years, in spite of every good intention.

This is partly because they are trained separately, speak different languages, perhaps respect each other too much. Both professions have become very specialised, and have been subject to opposing pressures. Artists have to conform to the cult of personality, the gallery treadmill: they have continually to astonish, and their images have a rapid turnover. While this also applies to a few stars, most architects work to a slower rhythm, and the pressure has been towards teamwork and anonymity. Few architects find it possible to be continuously original on tight budgets and with the well worn programmes that form the basis of most building work. It is also unnecessary. All that is required is to be literate.

When an artist is involved at the beginning of an architectural problem, at the conceptual stage, he is seldom aware of the many factors that have to be synthesised before the building takes its form: problems of cost, circulation, services, the nature of the site, its limitations, exposure and surroundings. Modern buildings go through a tremendous amount of research and committee decision making, and the elevations are usually the last elements to be resolved. Modern buildings are designed, and judged, almost entirely in the spirit of 'form follows function'. In such a world the artist is far from at home, and even the architect finds himself, on large projects, a co-ordinator of specialist engineers. Because he has rejected the role of stylistic cosmetician, the architect now wants to use structure, services and the rest, as a means to an architecture. He uses the forms thrown up by the technical analysis to make the building itself: to drag from the problem a kind of poetry. In this process the artist seems somehow irrelevant.

Yet he is not, because of the nature of the scale at which he operates. An artist works close to; his objects are made to be touched, or seen at close range. They are made by hand. Their relevance is a personal thing. A work of art is a *work* and it is aimed at the psyche. It has its own scale, the scale of the hand, the scale of a man standing. The work has a range of influence, seldom more than forty feet.

The scale of a man standing — Epstein's group at Bowater House, London.
Left: the scale of a man walking — the Seagram Building, New York by Mies van der Rohe and Philip Johnson

Sculpture and architecture : the building as a backcloth – St Pauls, London.
Below : beyond 400 feet the largest building becomes part of the environment – Brasilia. *Photo Architectural Association Journal*

Yet this is the range at which architecture only begins to operate upon the senses. Architecture is a matter of spaces and volumes, 'the skilful, accurate and magnificent play of masses seen in light'. These relationships can only be appreciated by walking within the complex of shapes and volumes (one reason why architectural models are so insipid) and here once again there is a quite definite limit to the size that can be comprehended : up to, perhaps, 400 ft. Beyond that even large buildings are merely part of the environment. This is the architect's scale, the scale of a man walking.

The next scale is that of the planner ; the ensemble of buildings, the scale of a man riding.

As the scale progressively increases, so does the originator's control over the final object diminish. The artist makes his object directly, with his own hands, and makes all the decisions himself. He is *responsible*. (Though he enjoys a reputation for irresponsibility.) The architect produces not the object, but a set of drawings from which a number of other persons will make the building. Should he be a successful practitioner, a large office will intervene between him and the drawings, and in any case decisions are shared with the client, the consultants and the planners.

The planner is so far from the reality of building that it's nothing short of a miracle when any piece of planning is actually realised. His task is to co-ordinate a mass of requirements and political decisions, about population, industry, traffic, leisure, education etc. into some kind of orderly pattern that might be realised by the architect ; or rather by a number of architects working at different times in different places.

It follows that the nature of the work of artist, architect and planner is fundamentally linked by problems of time, scale and complexity, into a coherent hierarchy of responsibility for visual order.

Decisions by planners are general decisions ; by architects and artists, progressively particular decisions. The work becomes therefore progressively more concentrated, intense and meaningful the further down the scale you go, and the closer you approach the scale of man.

Art as celebration: the 'L'Aubette' Bar, Strasburg by Theo van Doesburg and (below) IUA Congress buildings, London 1961 by Theo Crosby. Edward Wright, Kenneth and Mary Martin, Anthony Hill, William Turnbull, John Ernest and many other artists collaborated. *Photos H. Snoek*

It is at this scale that the wear and tear of daily life takes place. Places, things (and people) are eroded by time, and the turnover of objects is highest as the scale decreases. Works of art, even buildings, are subject to change through time. In this sense the work of art is expendable. The artist must allow for this, treat his work with perhaps somewhat less than his usual reverence, more as a celebration, an occasion.

In the context of contemporary building techniques the artist's problem is fundamentally different from that of the past. Until the nineteenth century the artist used the same materials as the builder: wood, stone, plaster, bronze, lead, terracotta, several kinds of paint. It was natural to add something to a building, using the same materials and techniques – to carve a keystone or a capital, or a sculpture in a pediment. Today buildings are made of steel, aluminium, glass and concrete. None of these materials are shaped by hand. They are manipulated by machines in factories, transported to the site and bolted together. A hand-wrought work attached to such an assemblage is usually out of key.

There are two possible solutions to the problem of integrating works of art in this new context. One is to make the artwork out of similar materials, and the same mechanical methods, and thus produce an object or image that by its concentration will express something complementary to the larger structure.* Here the danger is that the building will overwhelm the work of art by sheer size and volume. Yet a true integration is perhaps only possible in this way, and has on occasion occurred, particularly where the artist has been content to work in a more generalised way, diffusing his contribution through a space rather than concentrating on a single wall or object.

A sculpture in Devizes.
Below: entrance to the Chapel of Notre-Dame en Haut, Ronchamp by Le Corbusier

---

* 'Technically he must place the scale of his work just above the scale of the man who sees it, and indicate thereby the scale of the architecture with which it works. He must attach his work so tightly to the building, in similarity of proportion, material and technique, that, try as he may, the user cannot pry it loose (visually) and is thus forced to move through the sculpture or painting to the building, and of course, back down through it again to himself, experiencing in such unified, proportional relationships the place of all forms of our cosmic entity. In this way, a true effort toward the *spirit* is accomplished and the building becomes alive as a work of art'.
Mr Richard Lippold 1963.

A more obvious mode is to create a work in opposition to the architecture: a concentration of energy which asserts human values in the face of the mechanised environment. Such a solution works best in the deadpan glass wall situation, but becomes more difficult in the case of a complex and expressionist architecture where the building itself is a large scale sculpture. Opposition is an excellent posture for an artist, and constant reminders of the human presence become more and more necessary in a progressively dehumanised environment. (Dehumanised not perhaps in scale, but in that impression of being assembled without human intervention, which modern buildings exude.)

Central to the problem of integration is the personal relation between planner and architect, architect and artist. Unless they be friends, understand each other's potentials and limitations, both sides will be disappointed. The architect must create the situation for the artist in the same way that the planner creates an opportunity for the architect. In an environmental situation, however, this is no simple chain of command; it is the interaction between the parties that produces the magic.

Sculpture by Bernard Meadows for the Trades Union Congress Building, London.
Left: dormitories at Yale by Eero Saarinen with concrete sculptures by Nivola largely integral with the buildings.
Right: Rockefeller Centre, New York. A golden Ariel dominates the plaza

1800

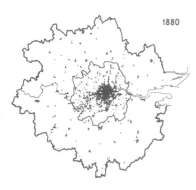

1880

1958

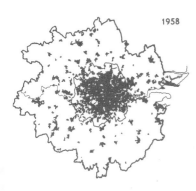

Three maps illustrating the growth of population in the London region

More people with more money

We are at the beginning of a period when population begins to press upon the world's resources. Until now there was always somewhere to go : continents to colonise, vast territories barely explored. Today these virgin lands are virgin no longer. Though great areas of open land remain, they are seldom productive enough to sustain the vast new populations that will soon be with us. The world's population of 2,7 billions is growing at 2% compound per annum and will double in fifty years. While most of this increase takes place in Asia, Africa and South America, in comparatively primitive conditions, there is still a tremendous population rise in the affluent areas of Europe and North America. In Britain alone the population will rise from 50 millions to 60 millions by 2000, and in the South East area there is an expected increase of 4 millions in the same period. That is, about 35% increase in 35 years. In the United States there will be 300 m. people by 2000, a rise of almost 50%.

At the same time technology places ever-increasing quantities of energy at our disposal, and most of the technical problems involved in the survival of the larger population can be solved. The capacity, however, lies almost entirely within the already affluent countries, and the task is to deploy the new resources to the places where they are needed. We must also ensure that benefits are equally spread. Increasing productivity is no social gain if it enables only a minority (as in nineteenth-century Europe) or even a majority (as in twentieth-century U.S.A.) to enjoy a good life which others cannot share. Technical advances produce social problems of considerable complexity, outside the scope of this book, but we must assume that, for the survival of our society, the problems of distribution will be some day resolved. Here we are concerned with those countries where a beneficient technology has produced an affluent society.

In conditions of affluence, the demand for space – living, working and recreational space – is very much greater than in times of poverty. The combination of new populations and high expectations creates a planning and architectural problem without precedent. It is particularly difficult where the amount of land is limited, in Britain and Europe.

33

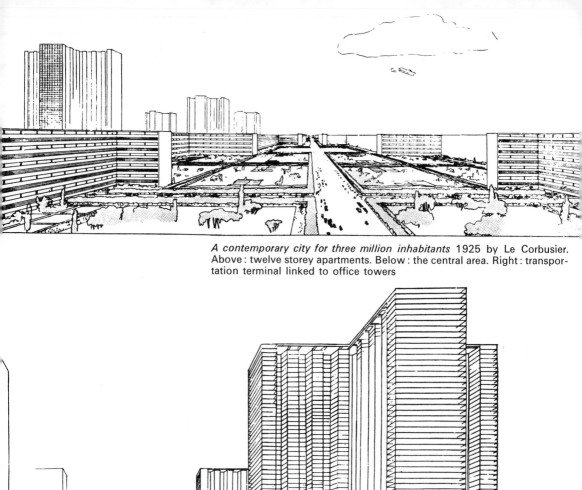

A contemporary city for three million inhabitants 1925 by Le Corbusier. Above : twelve storey apartments. Below : the central area. Right : transportation terminal linked to office towers

There can be no question of applying a little more of the same medicine (a modicum of control and a good deal of parliamentary talk about green belts, preservation and control of offices in central areas), when this has been conspicuously unsuccessful.

The problem is, quite simply, of a different order and requires solutions of another kind.

Complex solutions. The provision of shelter and an adequate place to work is only the beginning. In spite of, or perhaps because of, increasing numbers, people will want to choose where and how to live, how they are to spend their increasing earnings and leisure time. Above all they will want a structure and meaning in their environment that will reflect, and in part create, a structure and meaning in their lives. The influence of buildings and environment on people is incalculable, but we can all bear witness to its effectiveness. 'We make our buildings and then they make us.'

We could not offer a population 35% larger, and still growing, our present cities, strained as they are to breaking point. In a dozen years we expect 'saturation day', when central areas finally clog up with vehicles in all cities. We could not offer a countryside submerged in cheap housing and cheaper factories. We could not offer a heritage of old towns and fine buildings carelessly destroyed.

If we cannot bring ourselves to set to and build Le Corbusier's 'Radiant City' then we must at least rethink solutions in terms of what the problem is like *now*. The factors are increasing population and increasing affluence, with its natural concomitant of increasing mobility, leisure and aspiration. Unless we can provide for *all* these elements, we merely increase our social deficiencies. Le Corbusier put forward a group of solutions in the twenties, which are still largely relevant. He thought, above all, to realise the good life for all. This was to be found in a great city, with excellent communications, centralised office towers surrounded by parkland and high density housing. Factory estates, of course, were provided and so were satellite villages. Leisure time was to be devoted to sport, or allotment gardening.

A square in Antwerp, shabby but harmonious.
Below: new housing outside Antwerp 1958.
Right: a project for Berlin by Walter Gropius 1930

The 'Radiant City' was a good, clean puritan vision; much of it, the separation of functions, the emphasis on transportation, the amount of parkland, has been absorbed into town planning orthodoxy.

Le Corbusier made three assumptions: the city would start on a clear site, communally owned; it would be built and operated according to a single plan; it would be a highly profitable undertaking. Experience with the British new towns has proved him correct. Communally owned and comprehensively planned, they are indeed highly profitable investments.

When it comes to examining what is to be done with existing cities, however, there are too many complexities for a simple bulldozer to solve. There are the inhabitants, and the existing buildings, some of immense value to our civilisation. While serious and intelligent men are prepared to pay £80 for a square foot of the City of London, that place will retain its value and attraction; and the owners (who also control so much else in the country) will ensure that the value increases rather than otherwise. Value is a fact which is usually glossed over in planning theory, because planners always assume that value can be transferred. And so it can, though seldom to the planners' advantage in a free society. For example the public purchase of a site (the London Pavilion at Piccadilly Circus) for an open space, very neatly transfers its value to the adjoining, privately owned sites.

A crucial factor in planning is therefore to ensure that the benefits of any development can be reaped by the developer and not by some fortunate bystander. If a developer, or a community, builds a road, a sewer, a school or any communal facility, then this raises local land values. The happy owner of a farm near a town, if allowed to build houses on his land, will make a profit infinitely larger than his plough would ever bring him, purely as a result of his geographical location or a legislative decision. He has therefore achieved a betterment of his situation, and might well be expected to contribute some of his profits to the community which created them. Similarly, if people have to be rehoused because of the installation of a public facility, they demand and receive compensation. To planners it seems reasonable that one should pay for the other.

The City of London: Throgmorton Street (above) adjacent to the Stock Exchange (left); right: typical pedestrian way; and (below) the changing pattern of city building

Planners therefore argue, in many different guises, and for several different versions of, communal ownership of the land, or at the least, for a betterment tax on the beneficiaries of public investment. Even the speculative developers have now come to realise that there is no other alternative, and it's therefore only a matter of a generation or two before it is accepted in Parliament.

But this still won't make the City of London less desirable. It is a *place* where things happen and it has become such a place for excellent geographic and historic reasons; and also for social reasons. Being a place where money is exchanged, its fabric is built ultimately on personal trust. A market demands an active and personal participation and this is reflected in the form of the City: tight, intricate, secretive, with endless opportunity for casual conversation and face-to-face meetings.

Yet, like the rest of our society, the City is changing; it reflects also the aggregation into larger units that characterises our society in other departments. When this process is complete, the market may be only a memory. But while it lasts it is a reality which extends into everyone's life. A million people move into central London every morning and retreat from it each night. This human tide has steadily increased for a century, and is unlikely to cease unless our way of life is drastically altered. We are unlikely to make a radical change. It would require a legal, social and financial revolution. In the same way we are unlikely to make drastic physical changes in our cities, by the ruthless cutting of urban motorways. Old cities, like old people, don't take very easily to drastic surgery. The patient usually dies after disembowelling.

In any case time is against us. It has taken twenty years to begin the reconstruction of the bomb cleared Barbican site in the City of London; at even an improved rate the reconstruction of London's central area will take very much longer. By then increased traffic and population will have overwhelmed us. There can be no sense in cutting urban motorways through city centres because, apart from the physical damage caused by the process, the traffic problem is only a small part of the complex process of regeneration.

Traffic

Traffic is not important. What is important is how people live. There is no gain in cutting a few minutes travelling time if the result is an unsatisfactory environment at the end of it. There is no gain in adequate parking for everybody if it involves a half mile walk across the asphalt to do your shopping. There is no sense in planning for traffic without planning even more intensively for people's other needs.

If we cannot accept, or afford, the destruction of our old cities to accommodate the reality of our aspirations we must establish a system of priorities.*

The first priority is that the motor car be reduced from a necessity to a luxury. Where everybody needs a car, to go to work, to shop, for simple errands, there can be no question of a city. The car demands space — road, turning, parking and servicing space, and more cars require more space than ever. The natural form of a community where the vehicle is used unintelligently is the spread out suburb, where low density absorbs the noise, fumes and danger. For examples of this type of community we don't have to cite California; it is a growing reality all round us.

Such a community produces few social gains: the men go elsewhere to work, children elsewhere to school, leaving a very specialised and conformist society of women and babies at home. There is hardly any shared experience, because there is very little social contact. It is all *private* life.

In any case in an already densely populated country (and soon all countries will be densely populated) it soon ceases to be practicable.

For the motor car to be reduced in status an adequate, or preferably more efficient, means of mobility must be found. We have reluctantly to admit that no other system gives door to door service, is such a pleasure to operate, is so cheap, flexible and efficient. Or rather it is all these things, provided that adequate investment is made in providing the infrastructure of roads, garaging and so on that is necessary to the system's functioning.

Urban motorway, Boston. *Photo Cement and Concrete Association*

* 'Traffic in Towns'. The Buchanan report establishes this proposition at considerable length.

Oxford Street, London.
Below: an illustration (from 'Traffic in Towns') of the kind of vehicle/
pedestrian segregation required

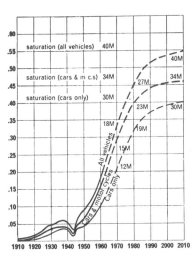

Graph showing the increase in motor vehicles predicted in Britain, from 'Traffic in Towns'

Piccadilly Circus, London

In the conditions that prevail at present in all the world's cities, the motor car has none of these advantages *if everyone had to use a car*. In fact, in cities like London and New York less than 10% of the population travel by car. In these cities the car *is* a luxury, because there is a relatively efficient public transport system. Many other cities either lack such a system, or have allowed it to decay. In London, for example, the pressure of private, and trade vehicles, seriously hampers the bus service in central areas, so that it has ceased to make a profit. The vicious circle of reduced services, more private cars, services further reduced, is already well advanced.

In any case the problem is compounded by the constantly increasing population. Most public transport systems are the products of nineteenth-century imagination and enterprise. They are not now as efficient as they might be, because sufficient investment in plant has not been made. Neither are they as quiet, elegant, spacious and comfortable as our affluent aspirations require. In short, public transport is overburdened and has become part of the 'public squalor/private luxury' dichotomy which is so hard to break in a society which distributes its gains in production to private citizens.

There is no doubt that to break the dilemma massive investments in a new infrastructure of motorways and public transport must be made, though we have seen that in densely built up central areas this is both uneconomic and unwise. Professor Buchanan's report 'Traffic in Towns' analyses an area of central London,* to show how the physical structure would have to be adapted to allow only 30% of the population to travel to work in their cars. He found that complete clearance and rebuilding would be necessary (and incidentally adjoining areas would have to be similarly treated). The cost and time required for such an operation are perhaps not unimaginable, but they are such that no government could seriously contemplate it. Particularly as the social gain would be so slight; a few more people would be able to drive to work and drive home again.

The investment is, therefore, unnecessary and impracticable in central areas, but it is required in those outlying suburbs without central area amenities. For example, the decaying inner suburbs

* Page 47.

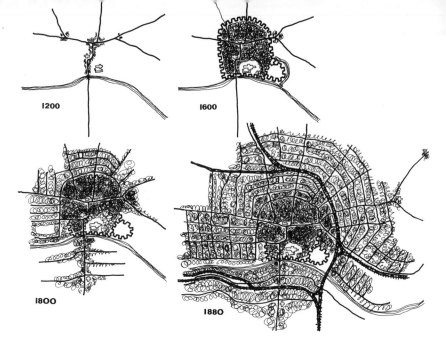

The growth of a typical though imaginary city, showing the ever increasing extension, and constant dependence on the old central area.
Right: Post-war legislation would enforce a green belt, more intense use within the city, and satellite estates outside

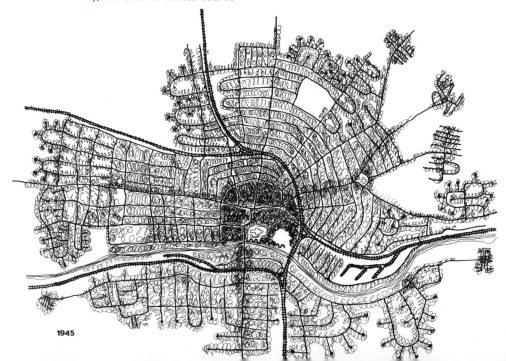

house vast numbers of people in obsolete conditions, and are themselves seldom of any intrinsic value. These areas require rebuilding, not as suburbs providing dormitory space for central area workers, but as integrated neighbourhoods with specialised central facilities. A devolution of offices and cultural buildings is necessary, partly to reduce the pressure on central areas, partly to restrain their continuous increase in value, but mostly to provide the missing elements in the subsidiary centres. An area with internal cohesion, that is, one that has something of every activity, will regenerate itself almost by definition, because it creates civic involvement. Such an area will retain its value, repay a massive investment in roads and services, and afford to repair its own damaged or decayed fabric. Because its activities are localised, it will contribute less to the movement to and from the centre.

Imagine therefore a federation of centres, rather than a single core with ever growing tentacles of housing or industry. In such a federation, communication between the new centres is even more important than between the old single centre and its suburbs. It is here that the new investment in infrastructure must be made, new rapid transit facilities. Securely integrated into the physical structure of the rebuilt area they help to generate the activity that supports and improves their subsequent performance.

The growth of cities in the last forty years has taken place almost exclusively in outlying areas. In London the 10–30 mile belt has absorbed the mass of new building and population; the centre has remained relatively static. In most American cities the spread is even wider; the centre has become almost depopulated.

There is no possibility of reversing this trend, or forcibly resettling the immigrants either by sending them back to town or on to other cities. These outer areas are now *urban* areas. All they lack is the urban infrastructure: facilities for a choice of work and play. The investment must be made here, and preferably now.

At present it is both practice and theory for both density and transport to radiate from the centre. There is no lateral communication, and in any case these outer areas are unrelievedly

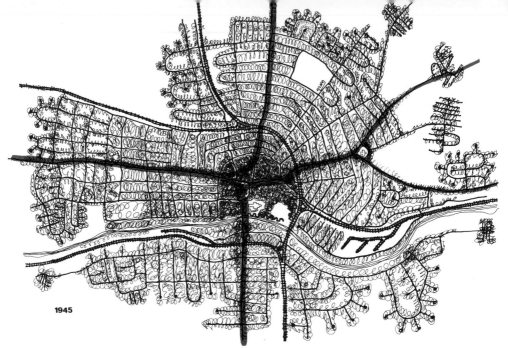

1945

The normal reaction to increased traffic is to widen streets, an inevitably inadequate solution which also destroys the existing environment.
Below: diagram showing the scale of road provision required, and how motorways divide cities into islands

1945

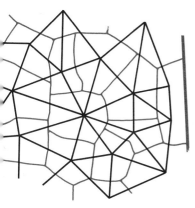

Once the city is considered as a series of islands divided by motorways, a rapid transit system links the federated centres together.
Below: A London Underground train

dreary: cheap housing, careless factories. Because land values are so high in the city centre, they here seem ridiculously low, so that land is carelessly used and often wasted. The time has come to take advantage of the relatively low cost of land in outlying suburbs to create new centres of attraction.

These will, naturally, lie at the intersection of public transport routes. Because they do, any investment in transport might be persuaded to pay off in the raised value of publicly owned land. But if this investment is made only in the form of a motorway, to enable the private car to move more freely, very little *property* value would be harvested from the investment.

To bring a motorway intersection into a centre, and use it as a node for development, would be a disaster in all dimensions. The space required for the intersection would be too large for any centre to compete with, and the traffic generated by commercial activity would play havoc with through traffic. Like rivers, motorways are boundaries, they create islands. The civic and commercial centre must fall within the island, and it depends largely on its intercommunication facilities with other centres. Easy connection to the boundary motorway is essential, but the key to effective development is an efficient rapid transit system. Provided always that the neighbourhood is specifically planned to allow it to *be* efficient. In any case a rapid transit system, with stops at 3–10 mile intervals works very well; shorter runs increase running times and costs.

Of the various rapid transit systems at present available everyone is familiar with railways, above or below ground. There are major disadvantages to this nineteenth-century invention. It is rigid, inflexible and extremely complex. Its capacity, because of safety requirements, is limited. The advances that have been made, or that are proposed, envisage electronic signalling, automatic control and driverless trains. These advances give the system a slightly greater capacity, but make it more complex, and do little to resolve the main disadvantages. The first is the fixed track with its constant maintenance requirements. Electric rails or overhead gear also require constant and skilled repair. Second, the block system permits only one train on a certain section of track, and thus inherently limits capacity. Third, it is inherently uneconomical to run, for example in commuter traffic, complete

Parking garage in New Haven by Paul Rudolph, a building type which forms a link between the vehicular and pedestrian realms.
Below: a conversion of railway lines into restricted motorways would increase passenger and freight capacity

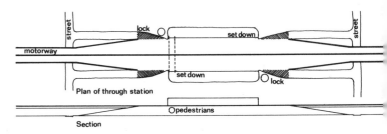

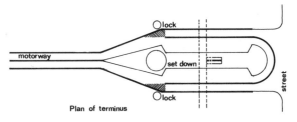

trains for a whole trip, while carriages are fully used for only part of the journey. This is because the system is not flexible enough to be finely adjusted to demand. Fourth, with regard to freight, door-to-door service requires at least two handlings. There is also a distressing tendency to use the railway wagons as cheap warehousing or storage.

The most talked-of alternative is the monorail, suspended from a tube housing the driving wheels, or running on a deep beam. The main advantage is that it is more economical to construct than a railway. The single carriages give a greater flexibility in use, and the system could be entirely automated to gear very closely to actual demand. Like the train it requires reasonably long intervals between stations for really economic operation: 3–10 mile intervals. The disadvantage, in spite of its high speed and relative comfort, is that it is a single purpose and inflexible system, good for certain commuter traffic, and nothing else. Its use would therefore tend to be restricted to large cities, and it also demands (as do all transport forms) a specialised form of city pattern.

The SAFEGE monorail car suspended from an overhead track. *Photo Taylor Woodrow*

Perhaps the simplest and most ingenious form of rapid transit, and one with many adherents, is the conversion of the existing railways into *restricted* motorways. The system is remarkably economical of capital expenditure (figures of one-tenth of current electrification costs are quoted) and it offers the flexibility that railways can never provide. The idea is to use the remarkable system of routes put together in the nineteenth century to form the railways, and to increase their capacity substantially by applying the twentieth-century invention, the motor vehicle. Railway tracks, because of the early low-powered locomotives, are built to constant levels and inclines are very slight. Given these tracks the performance of a modern bus would be remarkable; special vehicles could attain incredible standards of speed and safety. Rail routes are already organically tailored to increased traffic at major towns; the number of tracks have been multiplied to cope, so that many traffic lanes can be operated. Further, existing tracks have a built-in grade separation from all other traffic forms, the most expensive part of planning for the motor car. Instead of a constantly maintained steel track, with dangerous overhead cabling, the vehicles

would run on concrete road beds, needing very little repair. Each vehicle would have a driver, so that complex signals and other safety measures would not be required, though radar brakes and similar devices might be fitted.

The main advantage of the system would be in its flexibility of use. Vehicles could be directed, should demand require it, non-stop to distant stations, by-passing inner suburbs and stopping only in outer areas. Commuter vehicles would also be inter-changeable with main line buses, and could thus be easily standardised throughout the country. Freight could be hauled through the entire system, and literally taken door to door; the worst fault of present railway usage would thus be overcome. Mail, for instance, once sorted into special vehicles would drive to a station, pass through a lock on to the restricted motorway, and at the other end drive to a distribution office. The present chaos of bags on platforms would disappear.

Given such a system the existing rail routes could probably handle all public and freight transport, leaving the roads and motorways to private vehicles. The capacity of the system would be similar to that of a motorway: at least 1000 vehicles per lane per hour. Flexibility of use would ensure that each vehicle worked at or near capacity. The actual volume of material moved would be very large, and it would be safe, fast and comfortable.
'A city made for speed is made for success'. * To build a set of motorway routes while destroying a set of railway routes is an expensive recipe for failure.

---

* Le Corbusier *The City of Tomorrow.*

Christianapolis, an ordered community.
Below: downtown Manhattan, a profile as organic and as ruthless as a
tiger — a citadel of Mammon

Towards a new urban form

Urban form, once a fixation with geometry or anti-geometry is disregarded, depends mostly on means of access. That is, methods of access for visitors and servicing to buildings. As the motor car, and motor service vehicle, are a primary means, and there seems no reasonable alternative, the future layout of cities will depend utterly on our attitude to this vehicle, or something very like it. If we allow it access to all parts without restriction it will produce the squalor and sprawl which is our present condition. If we restrict its use, we deprive ourselves of a useful tool; take away its door-to-door capacity, and most of its virtue is lost.

This is a dilemma from which we can only be released by intelligence and money. Intelligence to plan and organise our environment to absorb the car, and use it for its unique qualities; money to make provision for protection and segregation from a dangerous vehicle.

'The Dream of the Good Life' attributed to Jacopo Zucchi. *Borghese Gallery, Rome*

We have been slow to realise that the speeds of a man walking, at 3–5 mph, are incompatible with the capacity of the most ordinary motor car, 40–80 mph. Because the motor vehicle's capability has grown slowly over the years, and at first did not seriously compete with the familiar horse, there was not the initial pressure for segregated tracks. This was the case with the railways, and is the main reason for the yearly railway accident rate being lower than the roads'. Railways are not inherently any safer, especially not to railway workers.

We have come to realise in the last few years, and particularly in the light of the projected increase in the number of motor vehicles, that segregation is essential, and basic, to any urban, or suburban, construction. Traffic generation, and its attendant dangers, is a factor of population density.

The planners' jargon word 'density' means the number of people per acre, usually residents. As a guide to the lay reader, most London rebuilding aims at 136 people per acre, inner areas are allowed to reach 200. Central area daytime (office) populations are often over 1000 per acre. In rehousing in New York the figure is usually 300. Really bad slums can go up to 1000, and places like Hong Kong often exceed that. Older suburbs in London now

The forms dictated by different densities of occupation — Harlow at 60 ppa.
Below: Kensington, London at over 200 ppa.
Right: Holborn, London, daytime occupancy at over 600 ppa. *Photos Aerofilms Ltd*

average about 100, having reduced themselves from about 200 in forty years, as housing conditions improved and young people moved out. No changes in the buildings have occurred; they are merely less densely occupied. The G.L.C. now calculates density at 1.1 per person per habitable room, so that there is a very precise theoretical correllation between the density and the volume of new buildings.

Suburban housing estates are generally based on the 12 houses per acre formula, that is, about 50 persons. The new towns vary from between 60 (Harlow) to 80 (Cumbernauld).

Private enterprise housing of the better class is as low as 20 ppa, and in the U.S.A. new subdivisions are very thinly spread indeed. To keep up value, and exclusiveness, some developers allow 2 acres per house (about 2 ppa), though this is extreme. Generally the $\frac{1}{4}$ acre plot, 16–20 ppa, is considered adequate for the stockbroking classes.

It will be seen that the fabric and texture of a city depends almost entirely on the density of the population, but there are several thresholds where one kind of environment must give way to another. For example at 25 ppa special provision for separation of vehicles and pedestrians, even by the provision of a pavement, is not essential. The number of encounters is too small to make the financial provision worth while. Similarly no special trouble need be taken to prevent overlooking between dwellings. On the other hand, a density as low as this is unable to support, within walking distance, any of the requirements of a civilised life: shopping, a restaurant, a cinema and so on.

The number of vehicle/pedestrian encounters increases as density goes up, and over 100 ppa it is a very real problem. Up to this density a system of horizontal segregation is possible and some reasonably sophisticated layouts have been put forward. Most are based on a separation of access systems: pedestrians in garden routes in front, cars in garage courts behind. People usually prefer the garage courts, and children find them much more interesting. The most intelligent contribution has come from Serge Chermayeff* who proposes a communal parking area, a lobby or 'lock' for post, trolleys, garbage etc., and then a close knit pedestrian system of court

* *Community & Privacy* Serge Chermayeff and Christopher Alexander.

Bethnal Green, London, 136 ppa. The photograph illustrates the changing modes of town development, from the original matrix of two storey terraces at bottom left, to four storey, pre-war, neo-Georgian courtyard blocks, to the post-war parallel slab blocks. In the centre Denys Lasdun's tower attempts to restore something of the intricate scale of the earliest buildings. In no case is provision made for vehicle storage or segregation. *Photo Architects Journal*

houses, with internal patios, and a certain amount of communal open space. The vehicle is at some remove from the dwelling, but the two scales are kept separate.

In densities up to 100 the vehicle is a necessity: access to communal activities requires that one owns a car, and, as density decreases, use it more and more often for every activity, no matter how trivial.

Densities between 100 and 200 are the typical planners' compromise. At this density the vehicle/pedestrian dilemma is insoluble, because the cost of providing the necessary vertical segregation, i.e. vehicles and people at different levels, cannot be spread over a sufficient number of people. Or at least not without a considerable, and, as we shall see, unnecessary subsidy. Most L.C.C. housing areas have been built since the war to a density of 136, a figure stemming from an apparently Orphic pronouncement by the late Sir Patrick Abercrombie. As the garage provision in these estates is usually negligible and in any case never more than 20% (with the result that today every open space is carpeted in Mini-Minors) it is obvious that traffic generation was never seriously considered. To-day few planners would advocate less than 100% provision, knowing it to be a bare minimum.

To provide car storage on this scale means that the housing pattern must be rethought, and that vertical segregation is basic. This in turn makes economic and architectural sense only if densities are somewhat higher, so that the cost of the new and expensive infrastructure of decks, pedestrian bridges and so on can be spread over the greatest number of ratepayers. Thus densities of 200–300 become not only possible, but almost obligatory.

There is no doubt that satisfactory dwellings can be designed, without excessive height, and in every way up to the highest standard of amenity, at densities up to 300 ppa. There is also no doubt that it takes a considerable amount of skill, so that a reasonable amount of sunlight reaches each dwelling, that people have privacy, open space and so on. The expensive provision of pedestrian decks and bridges allows for easy vehicular access to all dwellings, but the increase in density means that communal facilities can be supported by a very much

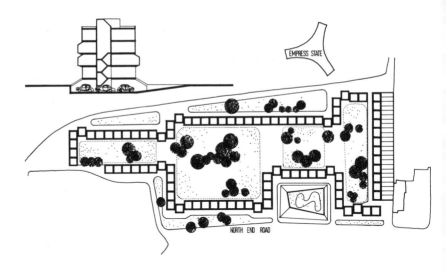

Two layouts from the *Fulham Study* showing an area developed at 136 ppa, to give the maximum amount of public open space and (below) the maximum amount of private garden area

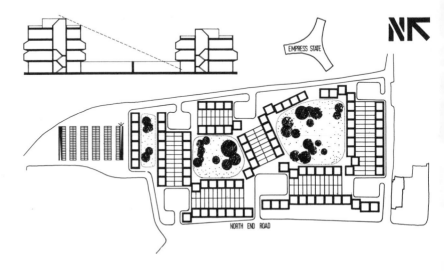

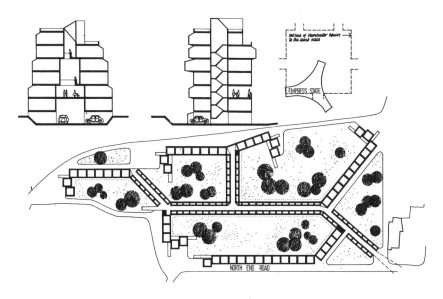

The same area developed to 200 ppa and (below) to 300 ppa. The size of the buildings and open spaces are approximately equivalent to Manchester Square, London

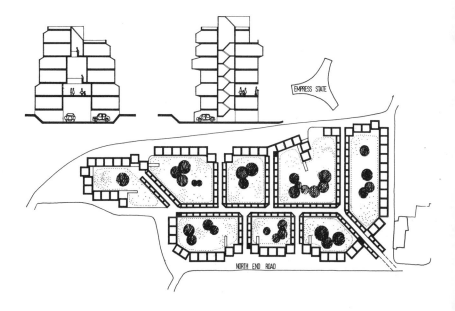

Manchester Square, London 1776.
Below: Georgian houses of different sizes, but conforming to a common aesthetic, make up a coherent environment by simple addition. The dwellings proposed in the *Fulham Study*, disposed in squares and terraces, are related closely to Georgian precedent

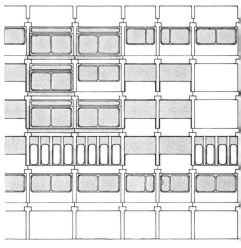

smaller area of housing. For example a 1 mile square of 250 ppa housing would contain over 40,000 people, the furthest $7\frac{1}{2}$ minutes walk from a quite substantial centre. Within this high density housing there would still be a great deal of public open space between the buildings.

It is only at reasonably high densities (200–300 ppa is the minimum) that the motor car is down graded to the status of a luxury. At this density you can choose to use a car, for a trip or a party; you don't *have* to use it.

Such a density also means that the network of public transport can be afforded, for it is only at high densities that rapid transit systems make economic sense.

A further argument for high density development is that if employment is provided, as it must be to give a social balance to the community, along with shops and schools, there is less necessity to travel large distances to work. Living and working locally increases social involvement, saves on transport. But this only makes sense if there is an adequate choice of employment, which again means at least 50,000 people in each cluster, with really good rapid transit links to at least ten other clusters. In the round figures loved by planners, the city of half a million inhabitants is theoretically entirely viable. That is, it can sustain every amenity of civilised society. And as leisure grows and increased provision is made for it, this figure will be lowered.

The pattern that emerges from the argument is that of clusters of highly concentrated building, separated by really open, recreational land, linked by rapid transit railways, restricted motorways or monorails. As much of the ground as necessary within the cluster is given up to car movement and storage, with links to the peripheral motorways, part of a regional and national system. The overall density of occupation of the area, including the recreational land, would be quite low. Certainly it need be no higher than the New Town standard. Now this is a nice tidy picture, and one very different from the reality of today. It is also at variance with a most powerful trend in our society, its permissive character. This stems from the relatively recent tradition of *laissez faire*, the right of each man to do as he wants

A new pedestrian precinct adjoining the flower market in Stockholm.
Below: new housing in Fulham, London. The residents are sitting on the
only public seats in the area, on a traffic roundabout

in any situation, first put forward as an apology for nineteenth century commercial practice, which has now permeated society. A society built on this principle is a selfish one, each man is an island. While only a small middle class lived by this attitude, the integrating factors of aristocratic responsibility, Christian charity and mutual aid among the poor could operate. Today all sections pretend to middle class morality, towards single family units rather than communities. Within the family dwelling can now be found every device to substitute for communal activity : the deep freeze instead of daily shopping, record players instead of concerts, telephones instead of personal contact. Most activities are now seen and followed more efficiently on television, rather than by active participation. There seems little need to leave one's home, one's mini-paradise, for any purpose whatsoever.

This is a social rather than a planning or architectural problem, and one might well be excused for ducking it. But my argument has hung from the single thread that contact with one's fellow men is in some way desirable and socially good, and that without it life is without flavour or meaning. Through even the most superficial contact, sharing a street or a bus, we can become aware of others – their condition, qualities, affluence or poverty. This awareness conditions and modifies our own behaviour and emotional growth.

An ideal shopping street – St Ives, Cornwall

The world seen through the mechanical eye of the BBC or the Independent Television Authority (or NBC and CBS) is both emasculated and frightening, very frightening. Yet in low density areas television is the only family activity, apart from a little gardening.* It provides a constant soothing pabulum, a world of dreams, with equally constant little reminders of how horrid the world is outside the cosy family circle.

It is obvious that such a device is as useful and as dangerous, in a social sense, as the motor car is in the physical world. Similarly it must be reduced in status to a luxury rather than a necessity.

This simply means that other, as amusing, leisure occupations must be made available, which will provide the necessary social

---

* A recent survey in the U.S. found that each American adult averaged four hours viewing each day.

A precedent for a system of pedestrian covered ways which might form the basis of future re-structuring of towns — Albany, Piccadilly, London. Right: Le Corbusier's famous diagram of the suburban dream, multiplied by two million

antidote. For these to be at all successful they must be accessible. Which doesn't mean a half mile walk on a wet pavement with a vehicular crossing every 100 yards. Here one can propose an architectural solution.

One might paraphrase Le Corbusier and say that a city made for access is made for success. In a climate such as the British a system of covered, heated and glazed access ways is long overdue, and with high densities they become an economic possibility. The pressure of population will keep them activated and safe. Given this system, the inertia that home-entertainment feeds on will be largely counteracted. If this accessibility is supplemented by municipal support for the arts and entertainments, such as is commonplace in most European countries, and eagerly canvassed in Britain by many organisations, one could imagine a lively communal life. In the light of the past fifty years' experience this may be difficult. But such a life, once established, is self-perpetuating, because it is built into the social and economic structure of the city. The city treasury provides the initial impetus and sufficient, constant backing to the activities, so that they are not dependent on the most commercially profitable kind. It would subside say, experimental theatre or an orchestra out of dance hall, bowling alley or public house profits.

In the same way quite elaborate public amenities can be financed from the rent of publicly owned shops and offices; but this is the subject of the next chapter.

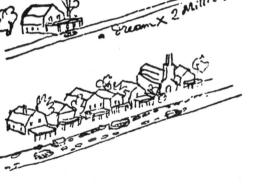

Office tower near the British Museum, London, typical of the dozens of major structures which will be making an unannounced appearance on the scene in the near future.
Right: an aspect of the 'private luxury/public squalor' dichotomy – street market in West London

Value

Architectural and planning theories always splinter on the insoluble problem of existing site values. Planners can seldom deploy actual money; their decisions may affect the value of people's land, but they have very little cash to invest on the community's behalf. The 1947 Town and Country Planning Act, which set up a planning ministry and the system of planning control which still largely prevails in Britain, provided a global sum of £300m for development rights throughout the country. This sum was to be paid as compensation to landowners who suffered loss owing to public development and enterprise. Conversely, owners who benefited from a change in use of their land (for example, from agricultural to building land, or from residential to office use) would pay a betterment tax. Given this financial control planners were in an excellent position to guide development positively. But in 1951 the Act was dismantled and the financial position restored.

The stage was set for the splendid and profitable drama of land and property speculation which we are still witnessing. Many millionaires later, we have begun to realise that something is wrong. Yet the major results of over ten years of happy dealing are still to show themselves. There are vast schemes afoot, in preliminary stages, in most cities; schemes that will change and petrify our environment for many years to come. Without a breath of publicity vast office blocks are beginning to appear, for example, in central London, creating immense and probably insoluble problems of traffic and pedestrian movement, to which the developers have made absolutely no contribution.

The only answer to this blatant exploitation is public control of building land, but the pattern of communal land acquisition is complicated with many checks and balances, and the process is both democratic and slow. The local or central government may buy land in the open market, like the speculative developers, and many authorities by early and far sighted investment are in a position to redevelop decayed areas. In this way land value can be manipulated for the public good.

Speculators know, however, how difficult the task of land assembly can be, and how a single obstinate owner can frustrate

Midtown Manhattan, uncontrolled real estate values produce a certain visual excitement at this concentration, but make for a poor environment. Below: a current alternative, new local authority subsidised, low density housing within 100 yards of a major west London shopping centre

A comprehensively developed area which has retained its value, Eaton Square, London 1827

a comprehensive development or siphon off its profitability. Local authorities have powers of compulsory purchase, but these are restricted to slum clearance, or where a genuine need can be proved. The local planner must be able to show at a public enquiry that his case for acquisition is watertight. This makes for caution, in the first place, and even then the procedure takes about three years after the first submission. It is a determined planner who can hang on to the concept, and all the details, for this period, and few planning authorities would care to handle more than one area at a time. This largely explains the failure of imaginative planning in recent years, but there is no clear legal or economic basis for redevelopment without the area in question being controlled by the developer. As only the local authority has the necessary power of compulsory purchase, and if its planners are to properly control development, it must own the freeholds in its area. This is the essential basis for planning, and compromises and partnerships in development can only begin when this primary point is implemented.

When the local authority owns the land it can develop it in a number of ways. By covering it with council houses at subsidised rents and low density, it can be sure of continuously losing the money of the ratepayers, and will always require grants from the central government. Though it might appear ridiculous this is actually the declared policy of almost all local authorities, and is encouraged by central government. The reason is, of course, the political problems inherent in rising rents, which have been the subject of political meddling for forty five years.

It is impossible to redevelop areas without the emergence, like it or not, of a clear rent structure, based on the value of the land and the cost of the buildings; and the rate and period at which the original capital was borrowed. This rent must inevitably be paid.

If an individual cannot pay an economic rent, then he must make this known to the local authority who should subsidise him until he can pay it. This might also encourage the local authority to help improve his earning capacity. The amount of subsidy is, in the end, what the community thinks it can afford. But to *build* a two tier society, council tenants *vs* private tenants or freeholders is socially unwise and undemocratic. People of every class

require dwellings that are elegant, spacious and which cater for their particular needs. The task of financing these dwellings is difficult only if it is attempted in isolation. As in all complex problems a simple answer (like paying a fixed rent) is only a part of the solution.

Cities actually *make* money, in vast quantities, almost by definition. This only means that the more profitable parts of city development have been given to the speculators, leaving the difficult and unprofitable part to the community. Fine for the speculators and their heirs, the insurance companies, but perhaps a little unfair to the community.

The ownership by the local authority of all the land in its area, and a share of the profits of the money-making sector, enables values to be equalised. Socially necessary but unprofitable elements, such as low income housing, might be subsidised by profitable ones. This can be done at even a fairly small scale, except that here it becomes more difficult to create a profitable sector.

It is here that the arguments for close knit, high density housing, developed at the same time as commercial, industrial and entertainment provision is made, become very strong. Land is thus used economically and by careful planning a dynamic social organism can be created. Because the housing areas in close association provide a guaranteed market, commercial rents and profits would be high. These would form an effective and growing subsidy for other uses. By making housing all high quality and single class (with individuals being subsidised according to their need) there is no social stigma or drop in land value. After the initial capital is repaid the continuing rents make subsidies mainly an academic matter.

Money borrowed for such a purpose, and on this scale could be at low interest and repayable over a relatively long period. This single factor would make for social and economic stability, and for large long term development profits.

This is a bald, and over simplified, account of a course of action that might literally recreate our cities. It is the kind of bait now held out to local authorities by the more intelligent developers, and therefore certainly contains both the qualities of practicability and profitability.

Shopping centre at Cowley, Oxford. Left: Crawley New Town. Though financially highly successful, the isolation of the centre, and the sprawl of low density housing, makes shopping burdensome. *Photo Aerofilms Ltd*

Hillside *barriada*, Lima, typical of shanty towns in all under-developed countries. *Photo Architectural Design*
Right: the growth of a house at Pampa el Ermitano, Lima, from the first invasion to its completion twenty years later. *Photos J. Turner and E. Levitus*

Action planning

British planning legislation of 1945–50 has long been the envy of the less civilised world. So long, in fact, that British planners, though wondering why the much vaunted system produces such poor results, are seldom open to suggestions from outside. The Town and Country Planning Act of 1945 and its principles have been one of our most prestigious exports; and developing countries have been able to try out our recipes in areas of rapid growth, with very mixed results.

In most cases urbanisation is taking place too rapidly for any coherent planning system; vast areas of shanty towns surround almost every tropical city. To bulldoze these areas has proved to be of little use, for the inhabitants soon come back again. To replace them with relatively expensive municipal or state subsidised housing is beyond the economic capacity of the country. Where this has been done on a tidal wave of oil, as in Venezuela, the resulting economic and social bankruptcy has been spectacular. Perhaps the only method which has shown any sort of hope has been to accept the slum and to promote the growth of a true city through self-help schemes and the social dynamic that they create.

For example, the *barriadas* of Lima are as bad as anywhere in South America, and official 'planning' can make little impact on the problem. Yet examined, as it were, from the underside, the *barriada* shows plenty of evidence of social dynamism. A group of squatters, with much proclamation and flag unfurling, take over a piece of land, subdivide it and help each other to build shacks of paper, canvas and tin. In time these give way, still by the same method of exchanging labour and materials, to more substantial houses. It is at this stage that elementary architectural advice, on orientation, provision for upper storeys, drainage, etc. is appreciated. At the end we may have what looks like a permanent slum, but because of its heroic origin, and the tradition of mutual aid, it is not really a slum. It is capable, given leadership, advice and judicial investment, of growing into a city.

In the same way the early ethnic slums of New York and London, overcrowded and unhealthy, were not like the chronic and

A London slum street 1962. *Photo Roger Mayne*
Below: new housing in New York in sixteen storey slabs.
Right: part of the west side of Manhattan Island, showing the new
scale of development, with isolated buildings

hopeless areas we know today. The East Side, Greenwich Village and Harlem, and Whitechapel and Bethnal Green, were at the turn of the century exciting places to live in, cradles of ambition and energy.* The lure of the romantic suburb caused the successful to move out, with unfortunate results. The community was deprived of its leaders, and thus lost its social dynamic, i.e. the capacity to renew itself, to hold the affection of its inhabitants.

Some existing slums are capable of regeneration, provided that a social dynamic can be created, or maintained. To take people from close packed row-houses and place them in seventeen storey blocks 600 ft. apart (as is a common practice in New York) has resulted in little *social* improvement. Delinquency rates go up and the new environment is soon reduced to the level of the old. What has happened is that the slums are no longer capable of growing, or able to retain their natural leaders; that is, those citizens who have made some kind of success and therefore exercise an almost unconscious control by civic example. Crude rehousing merely segregates the poor and weak, flushing their leaders and exemplars into middle class ghettoes of their own. No society can be stable, restrain its violent and criminal element, unless it is in a general way committed to law, order and a constructive way of life. It is the function of the planner to provide the format within which this commitment can be realised.

He must also be able to recognise those elements of our existing environment that are conducive to social growth. By protecting and extending these he will be able, often astonishingly, to revitalise a community without having to reach for his handy bulldozer.

---

* 'To him the streets of southern London are a scene of frolic, gaiety and extravagant adventure. They have to him a reality which the well kept avenues, bordered with trim houses, in which live the rich, can never possess . . . . . One night I walked with him in Los Angeles and presently our steps took us into the poorest quarter of the city. There were sordid tenement houses and the shabby, gaudy shops in which are sold the various goods that the poor buy from day to day. His face lit up and a buoyant tone came into his voice as he exclaimed : 'This is the real life, isn't it? All the rest is just sham'''. Somerset Maugham on Charlie Chaplin, *A Writers Notebook*.

Areas of London that have retained their environmental value – Belgravia and (below) Montpelier Square, though spoiled by car parking

For example many slum houses are clean, though communal services are inadequate. It is cheaper and more effective to improve the garbage collection service than condemn the dwellings.

Similarly the offering of loans and grants to individuals to improve their dwellings has more effect than transferring them to new, and more expensive, accommodation. It makes them responsible and keeps them near their friends.

A long lease is a much more socially binding device than a weekly tenancy, and emphasises the individual's worth and stability.

It is infinitely preferable to rehouse families in the same areas, even at very high densities, because it leaves unbroken the threads of social contact by which we all live. In this way the community largely avoids responsibility for the old (who remain in the family network) and benefits by their continued involvement in their families.

Segregation of the old, of wives, of classes and colours is a social evil; it is also our most used planning tool. It works constantly against that interaction of work, play, class and age group that creates a valid and dynamic society.

Park Avenue, New York, destroyed by its own social success

There are great areas in our present cities and towns which are excellent environments and which function efficiently. Usually they are the historic cores, or areas of eighteenth or nineteenth century building, such as Bloomshury or Edinburgh New Town. Because of their social success these areas attract development which seeks to capitalise on this value. Greenwich Village in New York, a social though hardly an architectural success, is the victim of intensive development which is destroying the very factors which have created the social value, the rich racial and functional mixture. Park Avenue, once a lively thoroughfare of hotels and apartments is now grim with banks and prestige-seeking office blocks.

In London, Chelsea, Soho and Mayfair, areas of immense charm and character, are the victims of their own success. All are irreparably damaged by prestige-seekers of various kinds. The original inhabitants move out because of higher rents and the areas are submerged – Chelsea by middle class pretension, Soho by vice and clip joints, Mayfair by offices.

Change over which the planner has little control: piecemeal rebuilding
and the destruction of a good existing environment — a square in Chelsea
and (below) a street in Central London

Mock Georgian terrace in Chelsea

Soho and (below) Park Lane, Mayfair

Areas such as these could and should be protected, by a simple blanket decision, for periods of twenty to thirty years. This would ease the lot of the planner and enable him to direct development into areas that require it. His position at present is ambivalent. He has little power to control traffic, or to forbid certain areas to motor vehicles. He has no power to prevent development of certain kinds even though he knows this might well destroy a valuable and unique environment. There is of course, in Britain, a system of listing buildings of historical or architectural interest, as well as much pressure to preserve them. This seldom extends to groups of buildings, streets or squares that, though without a specially distinctive building, still have immense, and irreplaceable, urban value. The preservation of these groups has also social value. They are identifying elements, provide landmarks; they are a link with the past and they give that clue to scale which is crucial in the kind of bulky development we contemplate with such equanimity today.

Good buildings, good urban and rural environments *must* be preserved, and well maintained. They are socially essential. That is, they create the kind of community we need: stable, civilised and constructive. The past is a growing point for the future.
When, however, a part of a city is thoroughly worn out and must be replaced, a vigorous and positive action is required.

In this situation the planners have come up against the time factor. Their methods are necessarily slow and analytical, and in highly urbanised and developed societies the pressure for change, for an outlet to the tremendous constructive energies of our technology, is almost irresistible. The planner is in the unhappy position of trying to hold a broad front, a whole city, against an army of wily and determined opponents, and almost single handed. He needs a new mode of action to survive.
There have been many proposals, almost all based on Sir William Holford's suggestion for corporations, like the governing bodies of the new towns, to tackle areas of existing cities requiring redevelopment. They would need powers of compulsory acquisition, and generous Treasury support. On completion of an area, they would hand over to an elected local authority.

Environments are worth preserving even though they might not contain outstanding buildings — Devizes.
Below: Marlborough.
Right: Knightsbridge, London

This is a great, splendid and above all practical proposal, for such a corporation could assemble the skills required. Existing local authorities often like to see themselves in this role, but always lack the financial, planning and architectural know-how to guarantee success, in a situation where a failure could be extremely expensive. Speculative developers, bloated with post war profits and short of sites to develop, but with a new found urge towards respectability, have begun to see a safe, though not perhaps spectacularly profitable, opportunity. If the authority will purchase the land under its compulsory powers, and lease it to the developer, the latter offers to build a comprehensive scheme, including housing, and to share the profits.

Our society has seen the growth of ever larger firms of builders and developers, so that it is only a matter of time before the market is shared between a few giant corporations. The situation is the same in the motor and aircraft industries, the banking and insurance world, the chemical and cotton industries, the glass business (where there is only one firm), the clay, cement or sugar industries and any other you might care to mention. In fact the construction industry has been one of the last to be absorbed into the oligarchic pattern, within the last twenty years. Such giants are easily controlled politically, and the present monopoly situation might be called nationalisation from below. All that remains is the need for a Treasury representative on the board. In these circumstances the builder/developer offers an alternative way towards implementing a community's needs, if no central leadership is given.

The developer must be directed to operate in a clearly defined area, of a size where technical resource can be brought into most effective action, and to work within a specific time period. This means, for today's technology, an area up to a mile square, with a minimum of 5000 dwellings and ancillary industry and services. It is only at this scale that something significant can be achieved, and the advantages of mechanised building methods can be realised. It is at this scale, 20–50,000 people, that a truly urban community can be created, in social and architectural terms.

The idea of taking such a small, defined area of an old city and creating in a short time a new urban totality has been called

A grand architectural concept has a profound influence on its inhabitants' way of life – Regents Park (above and right) even including the public open space, has an astonishingly high density.
Below: The Crescent and Circus at Bath. *Photos Aerofilms Ltd*

action planning* and this concept offers a way towards a truly twentieth century environment. Such areas must be rebuilt, and in such a way as to solve simultaneously a host of social, economic and environmental problems.

Firstly they must be rebuilt as islands, coherent quarters so that they can carry an image with which the citizen can identify himself. There are many historical precedents: Edinburgh New Town, Bath, Bloomsbury, places where a new and integrated vision of life was crystallised into a reality perfectly opposed to their obsolete mediaeval surroundings. It is only by an achievement on the scale of Regents Park that an environment of sufficient power is created to change the community's way of life. There is no doubt that these places exerted a profoundly civilising effect on their inhabitants, and they still do so — sophisticated sins, but no vulgar brawling.

To make a complicated social machine (like Regents Park) in the centre of an old city is a daring and difficult task; far more difficult than a simple clearance with a little more housing at 136 ppa. Like a chronometer, the parts are interlocked: uses, activities and formal harmonies, and the whole geared to a rhythm of movement of many different speeds. Such a machine can be constructed only if the planner is aware of every nuance of city life, and has in mind a vision of teeming, complex activity. Unless we make a virtue of increasing populations this single factor makes life a nightmare, a constant rearguard action against our fellow men, as we seek to hang on to our precious individual identities in infinitely spreading suburbia.

We must propose an incredible experiment: the revival of city life, the survival of social man.

---

* By Otto Koenigsberger.

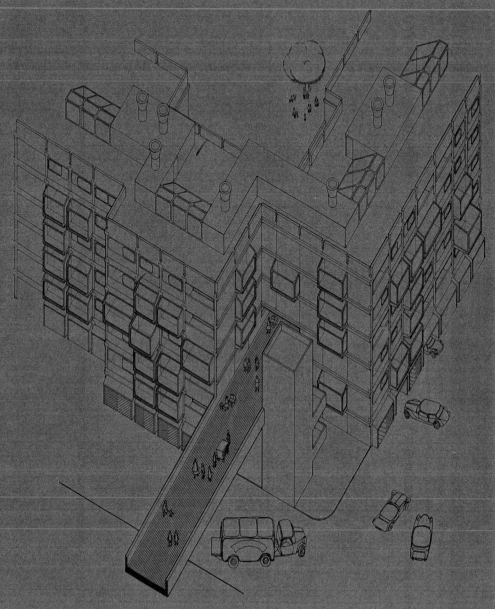

Housing system proposed in the *Fulham Study* — vehicles use ground level and are stored under the buildings. Access to all dwellings is by a second floor covered way, with staircases to an infinite variety of accommodation

Action building

There is no need to enlarge on the technical solutions to the creation of a community of 50,000 people in five years. One need only say that it can be done. Yet in the process one must affirm that, to be a successful shell for the next fifty years, the dwelling as we know it must be radically improved.

First, there must be more space. Present standards are minimal and in an affluent society space is the first requirement. Each person must have a room of his own.

Second, each dwelling must have a luxurious degree of privacy in relation to its neighbours – well insulated walls, minimal overlooking.

Third, each dwelling must be easily serviced, near to motor vehicle parking, and above all linked by a comprehensive pedestrian network of walks, bridges and galleries to a central area. Here there should be every possible kind of activity, recreation and speciality shopping, and a rapid transit station. Fourth, dwellings should be identifiable, individual, and cater for a complete range of family size and activity, without these having to be segregated into different blocks. For once housing is thought of as, say, a block of two bedroom flats, then people are immediately segregated into this family type, and they never meet a pensioner, or a bachelor or a mother of ten on their stairs. They are therefore socially so much the poorer. Given a flexible dwelling system people are able to move within the immediate neighbourhood as their family or economic circumstances change: as children grow up and move away, parents require less rooms, with no stairs. They should be able to do this without moving to another district, and thus losing their social contacts. Fifth, dwellings should generally be close to the ground, seldom higher than six storeys. Mothers in high buildings are unable to supervise children playing, and this promotes a chronic insecurity. Higher buildings require more open ground area, and result in windy anti-urban spaces between buildings.

To produce a dwelling system to fill these requirements is not impossible, to state the problem is most of the way to solving it.

There are many possible physical solutions, though it is fashionable to promote the cause of 'system building', that is,

Prefabricated building by the large panel method. *Photo Architectural Association Journal*

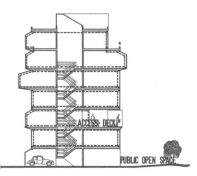

Section showing the Fulham proposals – second floor access deck which would be continuous over the redeveloped area; segregation of vehicles both horizontally and vertically

Prefabricated flats at Woolwich London. This trial contract required a minimum of 500 dwellings to be built to make the well-tried Danish Larsen-Neilsen system economic. *Photo Taylor Woodrow-Anglian Ltd*
Below: the Jesperson system, Denmark. *Photo Architectural Association Journal*
Right: compared to rocketry, building technology remains incredibly primitive

prefabrication systems which turn out standard dwellings by factory methods, with only assembly of parts being done on the site. All present systems are crude and more expensive than traditional building methods. The fault lies in the irreconcilability of flexibility and cost. Too many problems are attempted at the same time, with perhaps only one material, eg. the all-plastic house. The larger the unit part, the cheaper it is to make and erect, and also the less flexible in use.

What is required is a progressive standardisation of sizes and qualities of components, so that they become interchangeable, and geared to traditional usage. The problem then moves to the connections between components and this is where research on a vast scale is necessary. We need jointing and connector systems for an infinite number of materials and conditions, and also the capacity to make an architecture out of them. Traditional materials and systems allow this and it is only a matter of intelligence and energy to resolve the problems of non-traditional materials.

While one looks for an improvement and increasing sophistication in industrialised building, it must be realised that even to test a system, at least 1000 dwellings have to be built. At this rate we make very large mistakes. To make anything as complicated as the social machine previously described, we require an almost infinite dimensional flexibility of components, and very high performance standards. 'Systems' have an inherent tendency to extreme rigidity; that is, once the moulds are made for a particular dwelling, that dwelling is reproduced until the factory costs are covered and a profit made. While this is healthy enough for the producer (who invariably lives in a Tudor mansion), the social and architectural effect of these identical elements in the land and townscape can be imagined. They create precisely those pockets of deadness that are the opposite of city life. To bring something of the effort and intelligence that has produced the atomic submarine and the moon rocket to the problem would doubtless cost much trouble, worry and heartburn among the chiefs of staff. But as a civilisation we cannot afford to extend any single branch of technology very far out of phase with the rest; especially while most of humanity lives in mud huts, and even the more fortunate countries inhabit an environment of growing chaos and squalor.

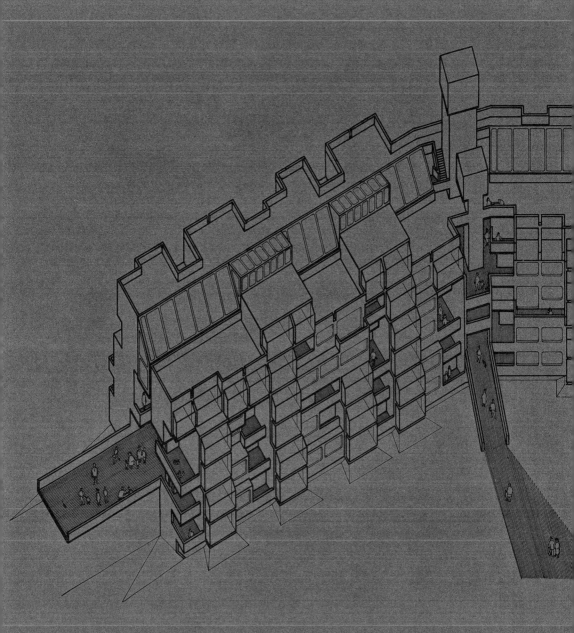

An alternative dwelling system developed in the *Fulham Study*, with an internal road and parking under the building. An infinite variety of accommodation is possible, all accessed from the second floor covered way

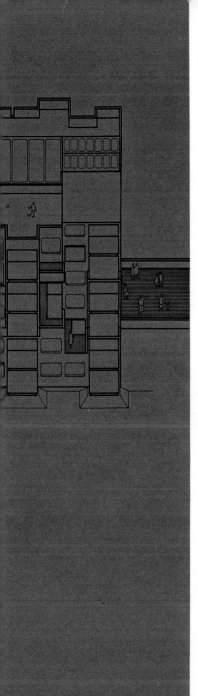

Towards a new environment

To summarise the previous argument, our cities cannot continue to expand, while feeding on the centres and infrastructure of roads, services and amenities of the eighteenth and nineteenth centuries. We must make a new series of centres for the suburbs, and grow them into cities, or elements of city.

We must make a new infrastructure of roads and public transport systems to feed and sustain the cities, to *serve* them.

To do this we must be able to manipulate land values, and to create new value, and the only basis on which this can be done is communal ownership of land. In this way the community reaps the fruit of its investment.

The new cities must be grown, as all successful cities of the past have grown, on a basis of social interaction and exchange. Everything in the city, its form and systems, should emphasise each person's responsibility for and dependance upon his neighbours. We are all *responsible* and to avoid social responsibility is an indication of social, moral and intellectual immaturity. In this sense, the new city can only grow out of what acceptance of social responsibility exists in old communities. Simple slum clearance and dispersal, the flushing out of the poor to make way for the middle class, is not social responsibility. To grow a community within a slum and at the same time physically transform it into a new world is the real challenge.

In any case the rapid change in the world's circumstances demands that the challenge be accepted. A more and more numerous population, with an even more rapidly growing technology at its disposal, now has aspirations to education and leisure that few have entertained in the past. A working week reduced to twelve hours is not very many decades away, and well within the economic life of our present construction. To provide an acceptable alternative to a degrading apathy and occasional violence, we must envisage a great increase in those elements of a city that deal with leisure time – outdoor activity and sport of all kinds, and, above all, education and art, endless specialisations and particular interests. These all require space and buildings: libraries, workshops, lecture-halls, laboratories

The central area of Cumbernauld will consist of a pedestrian deck, containing shops, housing and civic building above a massive motorway system, bus terminal and parking garage.
Left: The Economist group in St James Street, London by A and P Smithson, a piazza with three towers above the parking garage. *Photo M. Carapetian*

A street in Lindos, Rhodes, a continuous pedestrian system filled with visual excitement of which the Economist piazza is an equivalent, though only fragmentary, experience

and studios, aviaries and bandstands, practice-rooms and potteries. Today there is a tremendous pressure on these facilities, which are never adequately provided because they are minority interests and seldom commercially profitable. With more leisure these elements would become an increasingly important part of the infrastructure of the city. They would be life-giving elements in the desert terrain of existing towns and suburbs; they could form the growing points of the new city.

Imagine then a possible course of action: an inadequate or decayed area literally recreated. Dense housing grouped around a civic/office/entertainment centre and linked to it by covered ways which also sustain a varied and complex activity. A city of complexity, of specialised needs adequately fulfilled, with raised gardens, depressed roads, industry suitably tamed and integrated into the fabric. A city of quiet, insulated by comprehensive traffic separation. Motor cars and parking are built into the fabric, and the buildings act as insulation in the way that the houses of Greek villages are locked together to reduce earthquake shock; a city ringed with parks and gardens, bounded by motorways.

This recreated area would be a prototype, and would cost more than a few square miles of farm land layered with council or speculative housing. It would, in the short term, have to be subsidised. But here the disadvantages stop. In the long run, such a dream realised becomes economically dynamic, where the miles of suburb do not. It becomes a community, grows in value.

The effect of a positive gesture, a commitment to the future, is incalculable.

There is at present a great deal of talent available; in fact, some fragments of the dream have been built: the Barbican, the *Economist* building in London, certain University groups in Britain and the U.S., and many projects such as the Cumbernauld centre are soon to be realised. They are all fragments, tokens of tomorrow.

Industrial landscapes – Pittsburg.
Below: Corby. *Photo Architects, Journal*

Urban squalor: New York

Surely the time has come to tackle seriously the mess, carelessness and squalor of Britain's midland and northern cities, of London's decayed inner ring; the vast areas of Cleveland, Pittsburgh, Detroit. We must somehow direct the energies that, in themselves valuable, constructive and necessary, are making our cities a nightmare and our environment a desert.

Today we are beginning to realise, as we watch great areas disappear under waves of bad housing, the importance of a countryside untainted by the city or the compromises of suburbia, a landscape wild or cultivated, but not carelessly, haphazardly built over. The city is one thing, a place of dynamic activity, with its own restful periods, its parks and courts; the countryside is another, with its own rhythm and its own beauty. The two environments need and complement each other. For city people, the country is for recreation, for walking, camping, for weekend cottages. To accommodate all the leisure activity of even the next few years the country will have to absorb vast numbers of people and activities. For this we are quite unprepared. The demand for cottages, caravans, harbours, beaches is already insatiable. To this fantastic environmental problem there is no answer except a universal consciousness of environmental value. Until everyone is educated into awareness, the country will continue to be despoiled. This education, and legislation to help, must begin now. Successive governments have allowed almost every ministry compulsory powers in the countryside; there is only a handful of voluntary societies to protest at each new outrage.

In the same way provision for leisure, youth clubs, facilities for pensioners and so on have been left to voluntary effort.

In a society which constantly affirms its affluence this effort is negligible, as everyone assumes that the state takes care of these things. But ours is a *private* affluence, and government concern for the Youth Service or for the old is derisory. The Ministry of Education has built a single prototype youth club, the fruit of nearly twenty years of outside pressure and of the particularly outspoken Albemarle report. Inevitably social neglect and public indifference pays off in delinquency and aimlessness.

A society can only sustain an improving technology and high material aspirations if it uses its leisure creatively. Out of play comes the creative urge; out of social intercourse comes social concern. And that's what the city is about.

Selected bibliography

There is a vast literature about architecture and planning, though not a great deal about that borderline between them and sociology with which this book tries to deal. The truest and most moving is Jane Jacobs's *The Death and Life of Great American Cities*, to which I owe a great deal.

Architecture

Towards a New Architecture: Le Corbusier. Architectural Press, London 1946

Space, Time and Architecture: S. Giedion. Oxford University Press 1954

Theory and Design in the First Machine Age: P. Reyner Banham. Architectural Press, London 1960

Architectural Principles of the Age of Humanism: Rudolf Wittkower. The Warburg Institute, London 1949

The Earth, the Temple and the Gods: Vincent Scully. Yale University Press, New Haven 1962

The Theory of Proportion in Architecture: P. H. Scholfield. Cambridge University Press 1958

A Practical Handbook of Geometrical Composition and Design: M. Ghyka, Tiranti, London 1952

Changing Ideals in Modern Architecture: Peter Collins. Faber and Faber. London 1965

Planning

Garden Cities of Tomorrow: Ebenezer Howard. Faber and Faber, London 1945

The City of Tomorrow: Le Corbusier. Architectural Press, London 1947

The Image of the City: Kevin Lynch. Harvard University Press, 1960

Man Made America: Christopher Tunnard and Boris Pushkarev. Yale University Press, New Haven 1963

Cluster Development: William H. Whyte American Conservation Association, New York 1963

The Idea of a Town: Joseph Rykwert. G. van Saane, Hilversum 1963

Community and Privacy: Serge Chermayeff and Christopher Alexander. Doubleday, New York 1963

History Builds the Town: Arthur Korn. Lund Humphries, London 1953

The Nature of Cities: Ludwig Hilbersheimer. Paul Theobald & Co, Chicago 1955

Townscape: Gordon Cullen. Architectural Press, London 1961

The Exploding Metropolis: the Editors of *Fortune*. Time Inc. New York 1960

The Twilight of Cities: E. A. Gutkind. Macmillan, New York 1962

Traffic in Towns, the Buchanan Report. HMSO, London 1963

Planning for Man and Motor: Paul Ritter. Pergamon Press, Oxford 1964

95

Fulham Study: proposals for urban renewal in twilight areas, Taylor Woodrow, London 1963
The New Towns: Sir Frederick Osborn and Arnold Whittick. Leonard Hill, London 1963

Sociology
Cities in Flood: Peter Self. Faber and Faber, London 1961
London 2000: Peter Hall. Faber and Faber, London 1963
Towards a Habitable World: J. van Ettinger. Bouwcentrum, Rotterdam 1960
Nine Chains to the Moon: Buckminster Fuller. Southern Illinois University Press, Carbondale 1963
The Affluent Society: J. K. Galbraith. Penguin Books, London 1962
The Organisation Man: William H. Whyte. Penguin Books, London 1961
The Culture of Cities: Lewis Mumford. Secker and Warburg, London 1938
Technics and Civilisation: Lewis Mumford. Secker and Warburg, London 1934
The Condition of Man: Lewis Mumford. Secker and Warburg, London 1945
Mechanisation takes Command: S. Giedion. Oxford University Press, New York 1948
Greater London, edited by J. T. Coppock and Hugh C. Prince. Faber and Faber, London 1964
The Death and Life of Great American Cities: Jane Jacobs. Jonathan Cape, London 1961
Understanding Media, the Extensions of Man. Marshall McLuhan. Routledge & Kegan Paul, London 1964

Art
The Necessity of Art: Ernst Fischer. Penguin Books, London 1963
The Thinking Eye: Paul Klee. Lund Humphries, London 1961
The New Vision: fundamentals of design — painting, sculpture and architecture: L. Moholy-Nagy. Wittenborn, New York
Foundations of Modern Art: A. Ozenfant. Dover, New York 1952
Art in European Architecture: Paul Damaz. Rheinhold, New York 1956

Acknowledgements
Most of the background to this book was acquired through working on the *Fulham Study*, a report to the Minister of Housing on the redevelopment of twilight areas by the Taylor Woodrow Group; and I must acknowledge help and guidance from Harold McCue, the director in charge, and from Colin Hunt and John Topping, the team of architects: Ron Herron, Frank Linden, Peter Cook, George Gaits and Robin Middleton. The housing system proposed in the report originated in discussions for the CIAM Congress 1955, and the germ of the idea was published in *Architectural Design* in September of that year.
I am also grateful to many friends for encouragement and discussion, especially William H. Whyte in New York; and for a sharp and salutary meeting with Jane Jacobs. I hadn't read her book at the time.
Photographs on pages 21, 32, 74 and 94 are by Roger Mayne; on page 56 by Paul Watson. All other photographs, unless credited, are by the author.